Discovery

*See what great love the Father has
lavished on us, that we should be called
children of God! And that is what we are!*
—1 John 3:1

■ Many people know in their head that God loves them, but this truth hasn't found its way into their hearts.

That's how it was for us – Manfred and Esther. We had been Christians for many years and tried to live our lives accordingly. I (Manfred) followed a call into the ministry and became a pastor. We adopted three children from other countries and tried to be good parents. On our journey with God we experienced highs and lows. We had some gratifying as well as painful experiences.

A few years ago we both experienced – at slightly different times – a life crisis. During this time the foundations of our faith were tested. Influenced by a largely performance oriented and fear dominated view of God, we tried to please Him and earn His approval. We were faced with an increasing number of challenges in our family, our church, our health as well as inwardly. The expectations we put upon ourselves were hard to live up to.

We believed that God loved us and would carry us through difficult phases. That belonged to the category of theological beliefs that we never doubted. But reality felt completely different. God's love felt like it was extremely far away. What we believed until now, no longer gave us the strength we needed. During this time I (Esther) prayed nearly every day "let me be rooted and grounded in your love, understanding and comprehending its full dimensions" (inspired from Ephesians 3:17-18).

Our sincere desire was to have God touch us in a new and deeper way. At this low point in our lives He revealed His love to us as never before. We began to understand that God really does love and accept us as we are. A process began. This truth of God's love began to fill us. A lot that was bound up in us began to be released and relaxed. We received new courage and new hope.

Since then our understanding and experience of God's Father love keeps growing.

Because of this increasing revelation, our trust in God has deepened and sustains us through the difficult phases in our lives.

Over the course of the last few years we have discovered many practical ways which have helped us to allow God's love to travel from our heads to our hearts. In this Quadro, we have shared some of these practices, which have become very dear to us.

The first part includes some Biblical foundational truths about God's Father love and how that applies to us personally. In this section and throughout the Quadro, we have not only used scripture from the New Testament and the words of Jesus but also consciously included verses from the Old Testament as well as quotes from people who have experienced God as their Father.

The second part is about the liberating and healing effects that we experience the more we realize that we are unconditionally accepted and loved.

In the third part, we give ideas and suggestions about how we can receive and enjoy God's Father love in our everyday lives.

Finally, the fourth part is about how we can continue to grow into a lifestyle of living loved.

"God is love. Whoever lives in love lives in God, and God in him" (1 John 4:16). Love is the greatest. Abiding in God's love, and giving it further, is our first and highest calling.

Our wish for you is that this Quadro will be an inspiration to help get you started as well as being an encouragement for you along your journey into discovering and experiencing more and more of the Father love of God.

Esther u. Manfred Lanz

—Esther and Manfred Lanz

■ We developed this Quadro together, however, when "I" is used, it usually refers to Manfred.

How to use this book

■ This Quadro is divided into 28 chapters. It can be used for 4 weeks as a daily inspiration and encouragement.

■ It may be helpful to read this Quadro together with your partner, friend, or in a group. That would give you the opportunity to discuss it with others. You may discover that the different points will then become clearer and have a longer lasting influence.

■ We have quoted Bible passages from different translations. Try reading the passages again for yourself, maybe in a different translation and in the full context.

■ When you write something, you solidify it. For that reason we encourage you to write down the answers to the questions and take notes how you would like to put the practical inspirations into practice.

■ Whoever consumes passively remains passive. After each reading, ask yourself: If I were to tell someone what spoke to me the most from what I just read, what would I tell them?

■ Take time to talk to God or to others about what you have read. Through talking about it, it will become more concrete in your thoughts and you will be able to remember it better.

■ The "question" and "practical inspiration" at the end of each segment are there to help stimulate new thoughts and to encourage you to try new ways of doing things. They may help you to be open for new experiences.

■ Change does not happen overnight. In order that the Love of God can sink deeper into your heart a longer process is usually necessary. For that reason we encourage you not to hurry and not to put yourself under pressure.

■ Hold your heart before the Lord so He can continually fill it with His love.

■ Take time to dream. Picture in your mind what influence it will have in your life when you understand more fully how much the Father loves you. Ask the Lord that this dream not remain just a dream but become a reality.

Week 1
Discover Fatherly love

God is love

■ *"God is love!"* (1 John 4,16). This is a
unique statement of the Gospel that can
be found in no other religion in the world.
God does not love because He finds something or someone worthy of love. God
loves because His distinct eternal nature
is love. His love for us is not dependent on
what *we* are; it is based upon what *He* is.

The triune God gives us an idea of what
He is really like. Rationally, we can never
truly understand God's trinity. But as we
look at this love it can open our heart to
its reality.

God, the One that is love, exists in the form
of three "persons" – Father, Son and Holy
Spirit. They relate to one another in perfect
love. How breathtakingly beautiful! In the
center of the universe is a love relationship.
This loving triune God created man with the
desire that mankind reflects and returns
this love. He is looking for those that will
live in a loving relationship with Him.

Their lives in turn will draw others into a
love relationship with Him.

To better understand this intimate relationship the Bible uses different illustra-
tions. It is compared to the closest and
most trusted relationships on earth, like
the relationships between a husband and
wife, parent and child, and among friends.
God Himself wants to be our Lover, our Father and Friend. As we receive His love we
are enabled to return His love, as well as
love ourselves and others.

■ **Time to think**
What do you think and how do you feel
when you hear the statement, "God is
love."

■ **Time to act**
Talk to God about your thoughts and
feelings.

Abba Father

If you want to touch God's heart, use the name he loves to hear. Call Him Father.
—Max Lucado

■ Jesus introduced us to God as a loving Father. All that He said and did showed us the true character of God. With every word, every touch and every healing, Jesus perfectly reflected his Father in heaven. Because of this He could say, *"He who has seen me has seen my Father"* (John 14:9).

Jesus became the visible Father heart of God. His death on the cross eliminates any doubt of our value to Him and to his Father. "I, your Father, am for you – not against you! I have not come to confront you with your mistakes or to condemn you. I have come to remove anything that is standing between us and to draw you close to Me."

When the Father gave us Jesus, in a sense He tore his heart from His body. That is how much He loves us and wants to be near us. Through His Son, everything that has separated us from Him has been removed. Jesus brought the Father near to us.

The way to God is no longer found through religious rituals or by obeying rules. Instead we now become children of God through faith (see John 1:12). We can now call him "Abba," which means "daddy" or "papa". *"Because you are sons, God sent the Spirit of his Son into our hearts, the Spirit who calls out, 'Abba, Father'"* (Galatians 4:6). Our heavenly Father is touched in the same way as an earthly father when we speak to Him in this way.

■ **Time to think**
How do you feel when you call God "Abba, loving Papa"?

■ **Time to act**
Write at least 10 characteristics that describe a good father. Start each sentence with "A good dad ..."

At home with the Father

■ The father is overjoyed! He has waited longingly for this day and it has finally arrived. His son, the one who left him, has returned. Full of love and tenderness the father embraces him. The son is presented with gifts: new clothes, shoes, a ring and the fatted calf has been slaughtered. All indications that he has been forgiven and welcomed back into the family.

Everyone is having a great time celebrating. Everyone that is, except for the older son who is working out in the fields. He is the opposite of his rebellious brother; he is conscientious, disciplined and obedient. By means of his good behavior and extreme diligence he tries to win the approval of his father. Now his brother, who has done nothing to deserve it, is receiving all the gifts. His reaction is one of anger and bitterness. We see that the "good" son doesn't really know his father's heart. The father's main interest isn't his son's performance, it is a loving relationship. He wants to be near his son.

The older son lived in his father's house, but he was never truly at home. That is the central message of the gospel. The children have turned away from their Father – either in rebellion (in the world) or through religion (in the field). Full of love the Father longs for our return. For this reason the Father sent Jesus who reconciles us to Himself. Jesus shows us the way home, where we are welcomed with open arms.

■ **Time to think**
How do you think the Father in heaven feels about you?

■ **Time to act**
Read the story of the two lost sons in Luke 15 with your focus on the father's heart.

The Lord your God is with you ... He will take great delight in you; in his love he will no longer rebuke you, but will rejoice over you with singing.
—*Zephaniah 3:17*

God rejoices over you

■ Imagine meeting with someone every day who is extremely critical of you. Whenever you are together he confronts you with another thing you did wrong. You think you can never meet his expectations and he is always judging you negatively. If you could avoid him completely you would. The dumb thing is if he's your boss.

Whereas a meeting with someone that is expecting you with joy would be totally different.

Imagine the person you are getting together with would have a totally positive attitude toward you. With every encounter He speaks words of appreciation and encouragement. After speaking with him you feel invigorated, strengthened, and confident. Surely you would feel like you could hardly wait to be with that person again.

The quality of our relationship to God depends largely on how we answer the question: "How does the Father feel when He thinks about me?"

When you believe He will intimidate and accuse you, you'll not voluntarily seek His presence. You will keep your distance and make contact with Him only when necessary. The more you allow your heart to believe that the Father loves you and rejoices over you, the more you will be drawn to Him. Your meetings with Him will become more honest and sincere. You'll like spending time with Him and enjoy spending time with Him more and more.

■ **Time to think**
What adjectives would you use to describe how God looks at you?

■ **Time to act**
Put "take great delight and rejoice over you" in your own words. What does God say when He sees you? Think about this today.

The Lord bless you and keep you; the Lord make his face shine on you and be gracious to you; the Lord turn his face toward you and give you peace.
—Number 6:24-26

God's face is shining on you

■ God's face is shining on you. He is looking graciously upon you. He turns to you with kindness and love. This is the description of God with which the priests are to continually encourage the children of Israel. The people should have a foundational view of God as One who turns toward them with eyes that are smiling. This assurance of His blessing also includes God's protection and His peace. In ancient times it was common to be able to predict the King's pronouncement of judgment by reading the expression on his face: an angry countenance meant death, whereas a friendly expression meant life (Proverbs 16:14-15). It is important to God that we see in His face what He thinks about us. He is for us not against us. He is with us, and He is rejoicing over us. His gaze upon His children is full of love and tender encouragement. His eyes are soothing and healing. David also knew this when he wrote, *when I awake, I will be satisfied with seeing your likeness* (Psalms 17:15).

He described the mutual effect of this eye contact. *They looked to Him and their faces shined with joy* (Psalms 34:5).

In Jesus, in what happened on the cross, in God's creation, in His word, we detect the shining face of God everywhere we look.

I experience that deeply when I meet someone with an unusually kind and warm-hearted expression. When I see their smile it's easy to imagine God's loving eyes.

■ **Time to think**

What do you need to be able to imagine that God's face is shining upon you?

■ **Time to act**

Observe the smile of a warm-hearted person today. Imagine that your Father in heaven is looking at you with even more love.

A friend of God

■ Abraham is known as the "Father of Faith". He had a special, close connection to God. The way he related to God epitomizes how God pictures our relationship with Him. For that reason, He describes Abraham as "the friend of God". God called Abraham his friend, although the way he lived was far from perfect. The Bible speaks openly about his weaknesses. But even when Abraham did something wrong, he didn't turn away from God. He was much more likely to let God find him and respond to Him. What was important to God was Abraham's trust. Because of that He shared His thoughts and plans with Him (Genesis 18:17).

Jesus called His disciples his friends: *"I no longer call you servants, because a servant does not know his master's business. Instead, I have called you friends, for everything that I learned from my Father I have made known to you"* (John 15:15).

A heart relationship is more important to Jesus than acts of service. He wants to be close to us more then He wants us to work for Him. He wants to reveal His Father's heart to us, a heart that is longing for His beloved children. God doesn't want to just be our Father; He also wants to be our friend. He wants to spend time with us and show us His plans. It is more important to Him that we like being with Him, enjoy His presence and trust Him, than everything else that we do for Him. When we have the gift of His friendship we will want to serve Him and to help others.

■ **Time to think**
What activities and commitments hinder you from spending time with God?

■ **Time to act**
Take a few minutes of quiet. Imagine Abba-Father is talking to you as His friend. What is He saying to you?

First and second love

then you will no longer require the impossible from human relationships.
—Oswald Chambers

■ God's love is the first love. Every intimate human love is, at the best, the second love. This includes the love of a husband and wife, to your own children, and between friends. Why is that? It's because the love of God is of a different quality. His love is the only reliable source for meeting the needs of our souls. His love stays the same throughout the ages eternally. His love is without requirements and is selfless. Nothing can shake His love for us.

On the other hand, love between humans fluctuates greatly. This love can be hurt: it has limits and is dependent on our feelings and situations. If our heart is filled with the first love, we can be at peace living with the imperfections of the second love. When not, there is the danger of making the second love your first love. We might ask too much of someone, placing unrealistic expectations and requirements on them. We then become disappointed, accusing, bitter and withdrawn. In our 31 years of marriage, we have often reached the limits of our own ability to love. Because of our shaping and hurts from the past, we have hurt or disappointed each other unintentionally.

Since we have discovered more of the Father heart of God, we are learning to let Him satisfy our longings. Our marriage has become more relaxed. When we are filled with God's love, we can increasingly release our expectations of each other. We can appreciate and enjoy what we have to give to one another in spite of our limitations.

■ **Time to think**
Who are you in danger of expecting too much from?

■ **Time to act**
Today try practicing letting go of your expectations and be thankful for every little kindness that is shown to you.

I am that I am

*Comparison is the end of happiness and
the beginning of discontentment.*
—Sören Kierkegaard

■ I have often compared myself to others. This longstanding habit caused me a lot of pain and impaired my development. There were always people around me that made me think: "That's how I should be. I should be able to do what they are doing. That is a character quality that I should have." When I looked at myself I saw my weaknesses, but when I looked at others I saw their strengths.

One day, in the middle of questioning myself God surprised me by saying to me: "Manfred, I am that I am! You are made in my image. Because of that, you can also say 'I am that I am.' Don't compare yourself to others. I don't compare you to anyone. In my eyes you are one of a kind. Come to peace with yourself, with your character and with your personality. Rest in My love. Be content with who you are. Be completely yourself!" This truth has increasingly set me free. I no longer need to inwardly question all I do. I no longer need to reject parts of my personality.

Experiencing God's acceptance and love has helped me to come to peace: peace with myself and with everything that makes me who I am. I am at peace with what has formed me. Things can be the way they are. I can increasingly accept the way things are and let go. Erasmus von Rotterdam (1466-1536) brought this all to a point with the following words: *"It is the highest point of happiness that a man is willing to be what he is."*

■ **Time to think**
What quality do others have that you often compare yourself with?

■ **Time to act**
Celebrate your originality. Do something good for yourself.

Good is good enough

Simplicity is the ultimate sophistication.
—Leonardo da Vinci

For a long time I looked for recognition through my performance and success. I defined myself by what I did and by my position. In order to compensate for what I believed to be my inferiorities, I wanted to be an especially good husband, father, pastor and leader. Average was not good enough. My life motto was "Good is not good enough. It must be very good."

This self-inflicted requirement influenced the way I saw God and my relationship to Him. Through my discipline and dedication I tried to prove that I was serious about my faith. I wanted to be sure God was satisfied with my performance. Even in my ministry, being a success was extremely important.

The inevitable happened: I couldn't satisfy my own expectations. I was increasingly overwhelmed and finally came to the end of my own strength.

In the middle of this crisis, God began to show me His Father heart. I discovered that He completely accepted me as I was.

It awakened in me a whole new feeling towards life. I understood: I am and always will be unconditionally loved by my heavenly Father. I don't need to earn his approval. I'm already ok in His eyes. Since then, I'm able to live much more relaxed and at peace. This has helped me to not only better accept myself but also the circumstances and people around me. I no longer need to be something special. I see it as a gift that I am allowed to be simple and imperfect. My new life motto is "good is good enough."

Time to think

What is released in you when you hear the sentence "Good is (not) good enough"?

Time to act

Decide to take three things that you do today and say, "good is good enough."

Be merciful to yourself

Be merciful, just as your Father is merciful.

—Luke 6:36

Christians should show mercy to all people, is a belief most of us hold in common. It's usually easy to do that with our friends or with people we like. It becomes more difficult to show mercy to people that criticize or hurt us.

Mercy often comes to an abrupt end when we need to apply it to ourselves. With others we are maybe able to come up with patience and understanding, but with ourselves we are extremely critical and judgmental. When we deal with ourselves harshly and without love, the Father's love can't reach our innermost being. Jesus' instruction to "be merciful" was to include everyone, including you.

While at a training seminar we painted a picture concerning a certain topic. When we were finished the instructor gave us these instructions. *"Step back and look at your artwork. You now have two possibilities. You can observe it through the eyes of a critical artist or through the eyes of a compassionate mother."*

This thought released something in me. Since that time I've been inspired to remember that I have the same opportunity when dealing with situations in my life. I can make a conscious choice. I often ask myself: am I viewing myself, who I am and what I'm doing, with destructive self-criticism or with life-giving compassion? The Father wants us to be merciful and that includes being merciful with ourselves. The more we are able to do this the more we can show mercy to others. (*"Love your neighbor as yourself."*)

■ **Time to think**
What helps you to be merciful with yourself?

■ **Time to act**
Look at what you are and what you do today through the eyes of a compassionate mother.

Safe and secure

Wrapped in the protective hands of God we are safe.

—Ernst Ferstl

■ King David from the Old Testament was confronted with innumerable challenges, battles and impossible situations. He was often persecuted, threatened, desperate and deserted. Knowing this makes the verse in Psalms 131:2 even more astonishing "But I have calmed and quieted my soul, like a weaned child with its mother; like a weaned child is my soul within me." Obviously David had found a way of finding peace in God, even when everything around him seemed out of control. The picture that he describes is so impressive: a perfectly satisfied, quieted, contented child lovingly held by his or her mother. That is how David felt in God. In Him, his soul was completely protected, safe and secure.

This Psalm is often a comfort to me when I am in the midst of conflicts or in difficult phases of my life. When I am hurt and feel rejected, or when I am captured by worries and fears, I long for the lightheartedness of a child. I long for an 'ideal world'.

This ideal world cannot be found in ourselves or in the circumstances around us but only in an encounter with God and His love.

Near to God – in the lap of the Father – is where you are completely safe and secure. By Him, we are always welcomed with open arms, even with and in fact, especially with, the things that weigh us down and hurt us. Here we will be loved, taken care of and protected. Here our hearts can come to peace.

■ **Time to think**

What thoughts often rob you of your peace? What feelings are attached to these thoughts?

■ **Time to act**

Put a shawl or a blanket around your shoulders. Let this picture of how the love of God envelopes you sink into your soul.

Rewarded in sleep

The greatest enemy to intimacy with God is our service to Him.
—Dallas Willard

■ If a spiritual awakening was the result of religious performance, we in Germany would have achieved that long ago. In spite of all the great efforts made by Christians, the churches are emptier than ever. Many churches are languishing or fighting for their existence. Christian workers are experiencing a burn out. A few years ago I was in this same situation.

Psalms 127 gives us a new perspective. "It is *useless*" is mentioned three times. The Psalmist is referring to working and struggling without God's blessing. Simply being busy does not lead to a more spiritual life, but rather to more frustration and weariness. Maybe the most important lesson for many of us Christians is: let God do it! He is the creator of life – in the natural and in the spiritual. Real life can't be manufactured.

For that reason Psalms 127 says *"He gives to His beloved even in his sleep"*. The Father gives to those that allow themselves to be loved and that love Him.

Fruit in our lives comes from intimacy, not activity. That applies to the relationship between a man and a woman, and also between God and man. Without nearness and intimacy there can be no new life formed. That God gives to us even in our sleep turns our whole rewards system upside down. Particularly in times when we come to peace and rest, God desires to be especially near to us. That is when we receive a blessing that can flow through us to others.

■ **Time to think**
Which activities hinder you from coming into a deeper relationship of trust in God?

■ **Time to act**
List in order of priority your plans for today. Now strike what is the least important and in its place take time for a meeting with the Father.

2.6

Peace in the storm

Sometimes God calms the storm, but sometimes God lets the storm rage and calms his child.

—Hans Peter Royer

A mighty storm is raging. Huge waves are slamming against the boat. It looks like the boat could sink any minute. The disciples are panicking. In the back part of the boat the scene is contrastingly different. Jesus is sound asleep. In the end it wasn't the roar of the sea that woke Him. It was the disciples' fearful shouting. Because of them, Jesus commanded the storm to be still. Immediately the sea was calm and an almost unreal kind of peace spread over the water.

One detail of the story deserves special attention: Jesus was sleeping with his head on a pillow. His peaceful, undisturbed sleep, in the middle of a life-threatening situation, was specifically brought into connection with a pillow. For us, pillows symbolize comfort, trust, being at home and relaxing. In the middle of a storm, Jesus could literally sleep like a baby. He was utterly and completely secure in God. The responsibility for His life and His well-being was nestled safely in the hands of His Father.

In our home hangs a picture of Jesus asleep in the boat. In this depiction there are two pillows, one for Jesus and the other for ...? We've interpreted the second pillow being there for the one who is longing for peace in the midst of a storm. It is an invitation to lay beside Jesus, trusting in God's protection. Too often we let the inward and outward storms of our everyday life rob us of peace. However, for every storm there is a pillow and we are allowed to use it!

Time to think

What storms in your everyday life are the ones that cause you the most worries and cares?

Time to act

Take a pillow and lay on it. Just imagine Jesus is laying in your storm beside you. Give Him your turmoil and receive His peace.

Strong or weak

But the Lord said, "My grace is all you need. Only when you are weak can everything be done completely by my power."

—Paul in 2 Corinthians 12:9

■ In the past I always wanted to be strong and successful. The feelings I had when I was weak were very similar to what I felt when I had failed. I went through a time of crisis in my life when I came to the end of all my strength. During that time I often meditated on the text in 2 Corinthians 12:7-10. I could identify myself so well with Paul. I was confronted daily with my own inabilities and weaknesses. I felt overwhelmed from all sides: from what I expected of myself, what others expected of me, challenging situations and from spiritual attacks.

The problems didn't just disappear through prayer. Instead, God used them to break my need to be strong. He used these problems to increase a longing for a deeper encounter with His Father heart. During this process it became very clear to me; the Father does not just add His strength to our strength. He rather gives us His strength and the assurance of His support when we give Him our weaknesses.

When we have a heart attitude of dependence and a readiness to receive, figuratively speaking we open a door to His heart. If our position is one of depending on our own strength and a desire to do things independently, the door closes. With this perspective it is easier to accept our own limitations. It's also easier to detect God's loving intentions when we are in the middle of difficult situations.

■ **Time to think**

How can you be successful at calmly accepting your weaknesses as you become aware of them?

■ **Time to act**

Talk to God about a weak point that you are especially ashamed or fearful of. Thank Him that He wants to be especially near to you in this weakness.

21

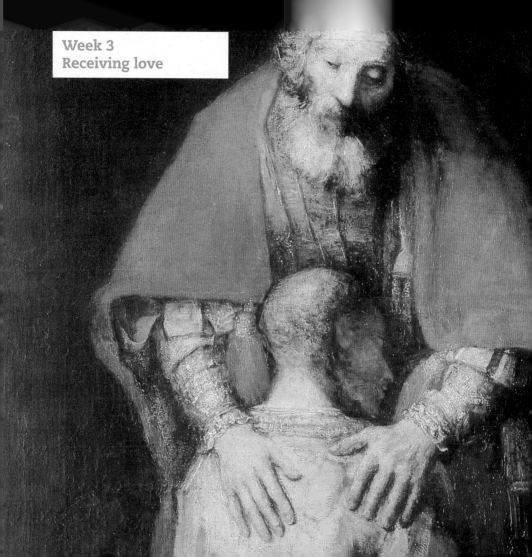

Heart communication

Genuine true prayer is nothing other than love.

—Augustinus

■ Prayer without really knowing God is strenuous. Real communication with Him doesn't take place when we grit our teeth and fulfill our prayerful duty, rather when we fall in love with Him.

My favorite definition of prayer is: sharing your heart with someone you love. Our Father is calling us to Himself – but not for a daily roll call during which we give information and receive orders from Him. In the past my quiet time was often strenuous and performance-oriented. I would ask myself: Have I prayed enough? Have I read my Bible enough? How long is enough?

The change came when it became clear: I didn't need to bring something to God but rather He wanted to give me something! Prayer is not some kind of tiresome obligation. It is much more a wonderful opportunity to enjoy His presence, allowing my heart to be satisfied with His love and goodness. This perspective awakens a yearning and a longing for Him.

The more I understand prayer as spending time with a loving heavenly Father and His Son Jesus, the more I am drawn to His presence.

Since then I have been set free from a fixed "quiet-time-system". I don't have a program that I have to finish to be able to fulfill my spiritual requirements or to appease my conscience. I just enjoy being together with God and sharing all that is in my heart with Him. I talk to Him about everything that is concerning me at the moment. When I meet with Him, I receive His love and give Him mine in return.

■ **Time to think** ————————
How can you change your "quiet time" so it will become more enjoyable for you?

■ **Time to act** ————————
Spend a few minutes in God's presence and enjoy His love and nearness without doing anything.

Our uniqueness and value are rooted in the fact that we are created in Gods image.

—Richard J. Foster

Finding your own way

■ We have three children and have a different relationship with each one. Not because we prefer one over the other but because they have such different personalities. Whereas one of our children enjoys physical closeness and touch another may enjoy it more when we express our love through practical help or a gift.

Over the years we have been able to discover many of our children's individual characteristics. This has helped us to understand their needs and how to best meet those needs.

Our Father in heaven has millions of children. Each one was created uniquely and has developed his own personality. Also in a relationship to God there's not a right way that fits to each person. Each one can find the way that fits him the best to relate to his Father in daily life.

The deciding thing is what draws me closer to Him? What helps me to intentionally receive and experience Gods presence and love?

One may love to intensely study the Bible while another would rather hear a sermon. Some experiences the presence of God in connection with other people. Others prefer times of solitude and quiet. Maybe your "place of meeting" is in the kitchen, the fitness or hobby room, yard or garden …

If we have are hearts tuned into God, He will come near to us and meet with us. The more we discover and accept our God-given individuality, the more we will be able to enjoy our relationship with Him.

■ **Time to think**
When do you feel happy and close to God?

■ **Time to act**
How and where would you like to meet with God today? Try out a new way.

Enjoy God

Taste and see that the Lord is good.
—Psalms 34:8

■ Georg Müller, a well-known "man of faith" gave a home to thousands of orphan children. In the midst of his many duties and challenges he never lost sight of life's real meaning, his relationship to God. After giving 40 years of intensive service for people that were suffering he explained how he kept his faith alive and his enjoyment of life:

"*I saw more clearly than ever, that the first great and primary business to which I ought to attend every day was, to have my soul happy in the Lord. The first thing to be concerned about was not, how much I might serve the Lord, how I might glorify the Lord; but how I might get my soul into a happy state, and how my inner man might be nourished.*"

Georg Müller took time every morning to read his Bible and meditate on what he had read. As a result his soul was deeply satisfied. This was the source of his joy and strength.

The prophet Jeremiah describes a similar experience: "*When your words came, I ate them; they were my joy and my heart's delight*" (Jeremiah 15:16).

The more we understand the character of God, the more important and precious what He says will become to us. The more we get to know the Father's loving heart, the more we will enjoy His words.

■ **Time to think**

What are your expectations when you encounter God and His Word?

■ **Time to act**

Look for a word of blessing from the Bible that speaks to you. Think about it often today and let it sink into your heart.

Soaking in His love

During the day, I consciously interrupt my work to relax in God's presence and enjoy His peace.

—Eva-Maria Admiral

■ Our posture influences our ability to receive. There are blessings that you can only really receive if you are sitting or laying down. That was Mary's experience as she sat at the feet of Jesus and absorbed every word He said. She didn't want to miss even one of His precious words. Jesus said that Mary had made the right choice, better than her sister Martha.

Martha was restless and distracted, busy serving Jesus. She didn't understand how Mary could just sit and listen. Martha's heart was not tuned in, so she had no reception. In the end she was left empty and frustrated (Luke 10:38-42).

We often feel the same. In our daily life it is sometimes hard to step out of the rat race and come to peace. It takes space and time to be able to receive the love of the Father. One practical way to practice this is often referred to as "soaking".

It could look like this: You relax and sit or lie down. You can also do this when you're traveling a longer distance by car or by train. Use quiet, possibly instrumental music to tune into God's soothing presence. Give to God your restless, anxious thoughts and imagine that you are immersed in an ocean of His love or sitting on His lap. Then open your heart to hear what He has to say to you, or remember words and thoughts from the Bible. Or just be with Him.

■ **Time to think**

What conditions do you need (time, place, music, peace, position, etc.) to be able to relax with God?

■ **Time to act**

Try it: spend your time with the Father lying down and listen to quiet worship music. Don't talk, just enjoy.

Listen and come to me, listen, and you will live.

—Isaiah 55:3

Listen to the voice of love

■ Words have power. Sometimes one little comment can influence our self-image for a long time. Children are especially sensitive to such formative words. If they continually hear comments like: "You're not able to do anything by yourself." or "Stop singing, I can't put up with it any longer." The results are debilitating and destructive.

The Australian family therapist, Steve Biddulph, describes such you-messages as programming. They sit firmly in our subconscious and help to form our personalities.

The words that the Father speaks to us sound completely different. They are encouraging, build us up and are full of understanding and significance. They do us good. We can accept them as truths that are meant for us personally. We can use them to powerfully oppose those internalized lies. This is also a process: Through continually listening to the voice of love, a healing transformation takes place in our self-image.

Scientific studies show that continually speaking positive confirmation and affirmation can change solid destructive brain structures. For that reason it is helpful to oppose the negative voices with the life giving words from the Lord. A few of these may be: "You are precious and valuable in my eyes, or I will supply everything you need, I am alive in you with My power and I will take care of you."

■ **Time to think**

What is a "typically you" sentence from your childhood that you feel still has you pinned down?

■ **Time to act**

Take this statement and replace it with a positive life giving statement that is in agreement with God's Word.

The book of memories

The value of a spiritual diary is that it serves as an aid to hear the quiet voice of God and to have fellowship with Him.
—Gordon MacDonald

■ In the Old Testament memorials were sometimes constructed after special events. For example once after Israel defeated their enemy, Samuel erected such a memorial stone and called it "Eben-Ezer (= Rock of help) and said *"Thus far the Lord has helped us"* (1 Samuel 7:12). Something that is comparable to this is our own "book of memories" – our journal.

In a notebook you can keep track of almost everything that was and is important to you in your relationship with the Father. To help with structuring your thoughts the following three questions may be of help:

1. What have I experienced with the Father? Where and how has He blessed me? What has He given to me and what problem has He helped me with? When you're going through difficult times it helps to read about how, in so many different situations you've experienced God's love and help in different ways. "Thus far the Lord has helped," encourages and gives new hope.

2. Where am I at right now? What weighs me down? What makes me happy? Writing it down can help you hold your heart intentionally before the Lord. You often experience a sense of relief when you write something down. In dialogue between yourself and God healing and release can take place.

3. What has the Father said? What truths has He unlocked for me? What words of love has He spoken to me? By letting these words of encouragement work in me, my heart will be touched anew.

■ **Time to think**
When you think about your walk with God up until now, what do you look back on with joy?

■ **Time to act**
Write your own Psalm in which you express to your Father your feelings of thankfulness, pain or love.

Encounters

> A Christian sees in the companionship of a fellow Christian a physical sign of the gracious presence of the triune God.
> —Dietrich Bonhoeffer

■ God loves to bless us through encounters with other people. At a conference, during a time of prayer, the guest speaker said to me: "Manfred, the Lord has a message for you". Then he took me in his arms, held me close and said "You are my beloved son in whom I am well pleased."

This simple but deep encounter became very meaningful to me. Sometimes the fact that I'm loved goes deeper in my heart when someone speaks these loving words to me out loud or when I feel the Father's loving embrace through the arms of a person.

When our "Abba-Way-Fellowship" meets there is always a time of sharing what is on our hearts. At this time each one has the opportunity to share how they are experiencing the love of the Father in their everyday life. We can talk about what processes we are going through or the new things we are discovering spiritually. These times of sharing often touch each of us deeply.

Through what the others tell about what they are experiencing with the Father, we all receive new inspiration and encouragement for our own journey with the Father. Now and then I'll take a few days and get away with a few men. We'll talk about ourselves and the deeper things in our hearts, for hours. Sometimes we'll talk about sensitive issues or hurts in our lives. While listening to God we pray intensely for one another. Whenever we experience these times together, the Presence of the Lord is so near we can feel it and He speaks to us in special ways.

■ **Time to think**
Through what people have you been blessed by God recently?

■ **Time to act**
Be especially aware today that God wants to meet you through other people. What did He say to you through them?

The key of "A"

■ Every instrument must be tuned to the same standard as the entire orchestra, otherwise, it will sound wrong, even if it is played perfectly and even if it is in tune with itself. Stringed instruments are especially sensitive. They often need to be re-tuned.

Our hearts are similar to this. Things happening around us, or our own mood swings can easily cause our hearts to become "out of tune." We are no longer living in harmony with ourselves. Sometimes we lose sight of the truth that we are our Father's beloved children. Then the strings of our heart need to be tuned again to the key of "A" like "Abba".

The Father in heaven wants us to continually hear the varied melodies of His love for us in our hearts. He wants to be in unison with us.

The simple words "Abba Father" can be enough to help us turn our hearts again toward God and remind us that we are loved (see Romans 8:15).

In our everyday life we can "hear" this key of A in different ways. It might be in a bird singing, a child's laugh, a touching song or an encounter with a loving person. It might also be through a word from the Bible or in the quietness of nature. When your ears are open you can hear the key of "Abba" everywhere and tune your heart again and again into the frequency of His love.

■ **Time to think**

What causes the strings of your heart to become out of tune? What helps you to re-tune them to "A"?

■ **Time to act**

Be especially aware of your heart today and try again and again to hear the tone "Abba".

Friendship with God

fellowship with Him. This is the real meaning of our lives.

—Brennan Manning

■ A child that is convinced of his parents love wants to share every joy and hurt with them. The better we get to know our heavenly Father, the more natural it will be for us to include Him in all of what we are experiencing in our lives. He is always ready to welcome us. He's happy when we express our appreciation and thanks to Him and always wants to hear about our dreams, challenges, or cares. He wants us to pour out our hearts to Him.

Enoch, in the Old Testament, had such a friendship with God. He was the first person, that the Bible says *"walked faithfully with God"* (Genesis 5:22-24). You could say he walked through life hand in hand with God, without having to consider all the rules and laws. Incidentally these laws were added much later through Moses.

Just as two people in love "walk" together – experiencing closeness, sharing their time, thoughts and feelings with each other – is how Enoch and God "walked" together.

That sounds simple and unspectacular. But it shows what was important to God then and is still important to Him today. He longs for people whose hearts are continually connected to Him and trust Him in every area of their life.

God was so delighted with Enoch that He took him to Himself in a supernatural way. In the New Testament his lifestyle is used as an example of faith (Hebrews 11:5-6). The Father is pleased with people that simply love and enjoy His presence.

■ **Time to think**

What would your relationship to God look like if there were no religious laws and standards?

■ **Time to act**

Take a walk with God and share your heart with Him just like you would with your best friend or loving father.

Balance

Jesus never experienced stress. He didn't rush from one appointment to the next, despite the fact that He had so many things to do. Although the needs and the pressures of those around Him deeply moved Him, He didn't allow his daily life to be ruled by these circumstances or by the people. He often went away to a solitary place and spent a lot of time alone with his Father.

This close relationship with his Father was His highest priority. This is how He described His way of life: *"I tell you the truth, the Son can do nothing by himself; he can do only what he sees his Father doing, because whatever the Father does the Son also does. For the Father loves the Son and shows him all he does"* (John 5:19-20).

Everything Jesus did was the result of a close relationship with his Father. What he received in secret he passed on publically. His lifestyle was the perfect balance between receiving and giving, hearing and speaking, rest and works.

We also only need to give what we have received. The one who is always active and serving without first being filled by God and built up by Him, will eventually burn out. For this reason times of quiet and getting away are so important. This is when the Father can lovingly minister to us. This is when we can receive His counsel in order to help others. Strengthened, we can then minister to them from a place of fullness and joy.

■ **Time to think**
What is the relationship between receiving and giving in your life?

■ **Time to act**
Before your next activity or meeting take a short time to receive God's love and counsel.

Do you love me?

■ Although Peter failed miserably in the last hours of Jesus' life, he still loved Him. But he didn't know it. The guilt and shame of having denied Jesus three times was overpowering. How could he ever even show his face to Him again? He was just about ready to give up everything and return to his old occupation. It was in this condition that he met Jesus. He asked Peter the same question three times, *"Do you love me?"* (John 21:15-17). There was no rebuke, no talk about his guilt, no working through it.

At the end he could only say, *"Lord, you know all things; you know that I love you."* For Peter it was important to know that Jesus hadn't given up on Him.

Apparently it was just as important to Jesus that Peter knew: Although I have failed and betrayed him, I still love Jesus. Jesus wanted Peter to realize this. He didn't want him to live with the self-image that he was a cowardly betrayer and a hopeless failure.

I can identify with Peter so well. Time and time again I think I don't love Jesus enough when I still sin or when I have bad thoughts.

When we belittle or condemn ourselves we are in danger of distancing ourselves from Jesus instead of trying to come close to Him. Then we need to become fully aware, "I am loved by Jesus"– in spite of my mistakes! And "I love Jesus – I really do."

■ **Time to think**

What are the situations that make you tend to turn your back on Jesus because you are ashamed?

■ **Time to act**

Let Jesus ask you the question, "Do you love me?" Write Him a letter in which you honestly express your thoughts and feelings.

Guard your heart

*Above all else, guard your heart,
for everything you do flows from it.*
—Proverbs 4:23

■ Our hearts are very precious to God. For that reason they are treasures that need to be well taken care of. The Father's desire for us is that we can live out of our heart, in unity with Him and with ourselves. Jesus came so that we can have a life of abundance.

When we lose the connection to our heart, we lose our balance, or point of orientation, our self and our strength to live. That's why it's important to ask yourself: What energizes me? What fills and satisfies my heart? What influences are good for me and which ones are not?

The human heart is sensitive and is easily unsettled by negative thoughts and experiences.

Attacks come from all sides: through cutting words, accusations, through difficult situations or hurtful experiences. Or sometimes it is our own inner voice that condemns us. If we give room to these things we run the risk of leaving the safe place of God's love.

In these situations the words from Franz von Sales (1567-1622) can be a great encouragement. *"When your heart wanders, bring it carefully back to where it belongs and place it gently in the presence of the Lord. When you have done nothing in your life except to bring your heart back into the presence of our Lord, although even after you have brought it back it still keeps running away, then you have lived your life successfully."*

■ **Time to think**
In which situations are you in danger of losing the connection to your heart?

■ **Time to act**
Take a heart, (e.g. a stuffed heart) very carefully and lovingly in your hands. Imagine that you are handling your own heart in exactly the same way.

> *In the end it all depends upon love: the love that I receive, the love with which I accept myself, and the love that I give to others.*
>
> —Kerstin Hack

Giving from abundance

■ Love has its origin in God and all love comes from Him. When we love, we are reflecting God's nature. *"Be imitators of God, as His dearly loved children. And walk in love"* (Ephesians 5:1-2).

The more we apprehend and comprehend that we, as God's children, are loved without measure, the more we will be able to return His love, love ourselves and love others.

In my daily life I repeatedly come to the end of my ability to love. Instead of being merciful, patient, and willing to forgive, I often react irritably, resentfully, and judgmentally. When I look closely I then become aware that I have lost sight of the fact that I am loved. Or, that I've not treated myself kindly. In order that love can flow through me, I need to be connected to the source. *"We love because He first loved us"* (1 John 4:19). Our love is in answer to God's love.

The more we receive and enjoy the Fathers love, the more generous we are in giving this love to others.

The more we give His love to others from a heart that is running over, the more the Father can re-fill our hearts with His love. *"Man, you have been created in the image of God who is love. With hands to give, with a heart to love, and with two arms that are just long enough to embrace another"* (Phil Bosmans).

■ **Time to think**

How do you know that your love tank is full? What kind of impact does that have on those that are around you?

■ **Time to act**

Show your love practically today. Take the opportunity to help someone, to embrace someone, or to speak encouragingly to someone.

Try something new

I can't be free, without loosing myself. I can't begin again, unless I recognize the necessity of ending the old.

—Hans-Joachim Eckstein

■ I learned this the hard way. Many years ago I was very upset to receive a bad grade and negative criticism about an essay I wrote for a German class. For decades this experience dissuaded me from putting my thoughts down on paper.

After my encounter with the Father heart of God a soft voice spoke to me, "Manfred, write a book about My love." I reacted immediately, following the pattern I had internalized. "I can't do that, I can't write." At the same time I felt a strong desire to not let these limitations restrict me any longer, but to step out into something new. I allowed myself to step out and try a new adventure. The result of this dialogue with my heavenly Father was my first book "Leben in der Liebe des Vaters" (Living in the Love of the Father).

Esther and I want to live increasingly like our heavenly Father's loved children: happy, playful, and free. We like to try new things: Although she is over 40 Esther began to play the violin and paint.

Recently I ventured into the rank of self-employment. Together we developed this Quadro. At the moment we are thoroughly enjoying a dance course. We look forward to everything that expands our borders and are eagerly anticipating the new things ahead.

Thank you that we could, to a certain extent, accompany you on your journey. We wish you all the best with many unique encounters with God.

■ **Time to think**
What inward limitations do you want to be free from? Through what thoughts do they express themselves?

■ **Time to act**
Try something new! Do something that you've always wanted to do, but have never allowed yourself try.

Don't forget

■ These thoughts and ideas have become important to me.
I never want to forget them!

. . . .
. . . .
. . . .
. . . .
. . . .

■ Along the way with my Father I want to practice the following:

. . . .
. . . .
. . . .
. . . .
. . . .

Book and Media Recommendations
- Jack Winter: Homecoming. Unconditional Love: Finding Your Place in the
  Father's Heart. YWAM Publishing, 1999
- Wayne Jacobsen: He Loves Me!: Learning to Live in the Father's Affection.
  Windblown Media, 2008
- www.fathersloveletter.com

We would enjoy hearing how you have experienced this Quadro.
Please send any correspondence to manfredundesther@t-online.de